THE FAVOR OF FORGIVENESS

Find Yourself Again (A Christian Devotional Collaboration)

DEVOTIONAL COLLABORATIONS   MICHAEL LACEY
MIRANDA J CHIVERS   C J WESTCOT   BECKY SIMS
ROBERT KAPEN   TANYA DUFFEY   KATIE ARTHUR
TAMBRY HARRIS   MATEJA STOLNIK VUGREK
LEENA J.   ERIN WATSON MOHR
NATALIE J. PICKERING, PHD   DVORA ELISHEVA
CHARIS MUSICK   CLARE JOHNSON

with
JACKIE PERSEGHETTI

with
AMI LOPER

Devo Writers

Copyright © 2021 by Michael Lacey with Story Builds Creative, Devo Writers Collaborations, and the Christian Writers' Collections.

All rights reserved. This book or any portion thereof may not be reproduced or used in any manner whatsoever without the express written permission of the publisher except for the use of brief quotations in a book review. Each author owns their content and can use it at their discretion via the shared contract.
Story Builds Creative
2680 Baptist Road, Nesbit, MS 38651
Story-Builds.com
DevoWriters.com

ISBN (ebook): 978-1-954838-08-6
ISBN (paperback): 978-1-954838-10-9

Cover design, formatting, and production by Michael Lacey with Story Builds Creative and Devo Writers Collaborations.

Contents

Preface	v
Special Thanks	vii
Introduction	ix
1. For-GIVE-ness *Michael Lacey*	1
2. Should We Forgive God? *Michael Lacey*	5
3. The Hardest Person to Forgive *Michael Lacey*	8
4. Forgive Before Offense *Michael Lacey*	11
5. For the Saving of Many *Michael Lacey*	14
6. The Prison *Ami Loper*	17
7. The Gift of Grief *Ami Loper*	21
8. Gila Monster Attack *Ami Loper*	24
9. How Do You Spell Relief? *Jackie Perseghetti*	27
10. The Art of Asking Forgiveness *Jackie Perseghetti*	30
11. Past Pretending *Jackie Perseghetti*	33
12. The (Un)chosen Yoke *Jackie Perseghetti*	36
13. When I Hide My Sin *Miranda J. Chivers*	39
14. When Nations Sin *Miranda J. Chivers*	43

15. Forgiving Myself — 46
Miranda J. Chivers

16. My Forgiveness Story — 49
Miranda J. Chivers

17. In the Midst of it All — 52
CJ Westcot

18. Healing through the Hurt — 56
CJ Westcot

19. Finding Grace in the Wounds — 59
CJ Westcot

20. Where Is God When Others Hurt Us? — 62
Tanya Duffey

21. Shedding the Weight — 65
Robert Kapen

22. Forgiveness, Humility, & Repentance — 68
Charis Musick

23. Healing Our Woundedness — 72
Tambry Harris

24. Between Friends — 76
Leena J

25. Hearts Can Change — 79
Mateja Stolnik Vugrek

26. The Prison of Unforgiveness — 82
Katie Arthur

27. The Forgiveness Quandary — 85
Erin Watson Mohr

28. The Spiraled Path of Forgiveness — 88
Dvora Elisheva

29. Confession — 91
Carrie Bevell Partridge

30. Lament. Accept. Then Forgive. — 94
Natalie K. Pickering, PhD, BCC, MISCP

31. Joseph: A Picture of God's Process — 98
Clare Johnson

Free Devotionals and Stories — 101
Are YOU a writer? — 103
Last Request — 105

Preface

The Favor of Forgiveness is a collection of devotions that can be read daily throughout the month. This collection is formed with various authors around the world. You may notice different spellings or styles such as "Savior" versus "Saviour". We celebrate the international feel and have retained author styles.

The viewpoints of each author do not reflect those of everyone involved. We differ on some theological issues, but our goal is to come together—despite those differences—to share messages that challenge us to be faithful through troubled times.

DISCLAIMER: if you have any issues with the theologies (which do vary slightly), or any devos in particular, please reach out to those authors directly. Each of us are passionate about the Word of God, and if we are risking blasphemy or causing damage in any way, we WANT to know. God's word is holy, and it deserves our best. Each writer is allowed to share their beliefs in a judgment-free way.

However, one core belief holds true for all of us: salvation (and thus eternity in heaven with God) is available to all who call upon the name of Jesus, as outlined in John 14:6 and John 3:16, of course.

May the real stories from these real people reflect the real God and help you receive the favor of forgiveness in your life.

You are not alone. You are loved. You are here for a reason.

Godspeed,

-Michael Lacey, Story-Builds.com (and the Devo Writers Collaborations group)

As per Amazon Affiliate rules: there are affiliate links to products in this book. As an Amazon Associate, we earn from qualifying purchases.

Special Thanks

A portion of the proceeds from each Devo Writers Collaboration goes to a related charity for the first year of each book release. By purchasing this devotional collection, you are supporting victims of COVID-19 and others who need our help through the Christian Relief Fund.

So, we collectively shout, "THANK YOU!" for your 'donation', and we have faith you will draw nearer to God through these heartfelt writings.

Introduction

Forgiveness is one of the hardest things to do in life yet one of the most important, if not the most important thing. If you were never forgiven, where would you be? And if you never forgive, how deep will the root of bitterness go and what will grow out of it? The pain from unforgiveness could one day be greater than the original offense.

Among the many powerful teachings from Jesus and the apostles, forgiveness is a consistent theme. Perhaps it's because forgiveness is an ongoing exercise, even daily. Did you realize that one of the main tenets of the Lord's Prayer—which is meant to be on a daily basis—is forgiveness?

> "This, then, is how you should pray: 'Our Father in heaven, hallowed be your name, your kingdom come, your will be done, on earth as it is in heaven. Give us today our daily bread. And forgive us our debts, as we

> also have forgiven our debtors. And lead us not into temptation, but deliver us from the evil one."

—Matthew: 6:9b-13

And there's as a word that stands out and is consistent among most translations: the word "as" in between the two extensions of forgiveness. What if that word doesn't just mean 'like', as in "walk as/like I do...in the same manner, temperament, etc." What if it also means something more consequential, like "while," "proportionate to," or "to the same extent."

It's possible the phrase simply means, "because" I forgive or "in those times I do forgive," but might mean the level of our extension of forgiveness could have a bearing on our being forgiven.

In that case, we may not be asking for any forgiveness on that day if we aren't willing to extend any! Consider the parable of the man who was forgiven a great debt only to hold his own lesser debtor to a punishment. The man who was forgiven but did not forgive ended up getting a punishment far worse.

I don't know about you, but wish to be fully forgiven daily, so I should grant that to those who have wronged me.

Now, I know that may not sit well with you, so I'll lean back into scripture. Directly following the Lord's Prayer, this is what Jesus said:

> "For if you forgive other people when they sin against you, your heavenly Father will also forgive you. But if

you do not forgive others their sins, your Father will not forgive your sins."

—Matthew 6:14-15 (NIV)

If you're still not convinced of the value of forgiveness on a daily basis, Ephesians sets the bar even higher. Consider the level to which God has forgiven you: completely! Now read this:

"Let all bitterness, anger and wrath, shouting and slander be removed from you, along with all malice. And be kind and compassionate to one another, forgiving one another, just as God also forgave you in Christ."

—Ephesians 4:31-32 (CSB)

So, to what extent should we forgive? As the Lord forgave you. In doing these things, we'll be allowing God to remove the roots of bitterness, anger and wrath, and shouting and slander. That is the incredible *favor of forgiveness.*

"For I consider that the sufferings of this present time are not worth comparing with the glory that is going to be revealed to us."

—Romans 8:18 (CSB)

Take time on a daily basis to go through these devotionals and lean into God's direction for your life personally. Allow these real stories from real people remind you of our very real God.

And when you've gone through this collection, go deeper by grabbing one of the other books in the series and also by tapping some of your favorite writer's links. We write because we are called to, but mostly we want to help. And many of our writers have incredible resources, writings, teachings, and offerings to help you through your own journey!

> *Lastly, if you're a writer—or even have an inclination to join something like this—go to DevoWriters.com to learn more about what we do and why.*

ONE

For-GIVE-ness

MICHAEL LACEY

"Even when it's hard, everything God asks us to do is ultimately for our good." —Joyce Meyer

One of the main issues with forgiving someone is feeling like they are 'getting away with it'. Before I got married, I tried speaking with my future wife's father on multiple occasions to ask for his blessing. He wouldn't return my calls, and when I went to his house, he literally slammed the door in my face. For a while, he wouldn't even start a conversation with me. The times I did speak with him, I don't think I'd ever been so physically and emotionally charged. And it didn't just hurt me, it hurt my future wife, his own daughter.

I will say that she may have harbored unforgiveness longer than I. You see, she has a deep desire for justice. There's not a pretty resolution to this story except that we act like all of that never happened. While I don't see the need to tell him to his face (that would be another devo right there—some people won't ever understand how they've hurt you), I have forgiven him. I don't have to understand any of it, though I try to sometimes.

Back to that desire for justice…does that sound familiar? Here's an interesting perspective: when we feel something deep inside, it's likely something informing us of not just a characteristic of ourselves but one of our Creator. Since we're created in God's image, this shows how deep His desire is for justice.

However, we also desire peace. So, which do you want more? Here's the problem: we can have the peace of God and allow Him to provide the justice, or we can try to take justice into our hands and never really find peace. That sounds like an easy choice, but we constantly choose not to forgive because it's not fair that someone would be "let off the hook," it's not just.

Forgiveness is not giving up, it's giving *it* up to God. It's taking it all out of your hands and putting it into His: the hurt, the repercussions and retribution, the healing. Forgiveness is part of our partnership with Jesus and is only made possible by cooperating with Jesus rather than seeking justification.

> "Just as the Lord has forgiven you, so you are also to forgive. Above all, put on love, which is the perfect bond of unity. And let the peace of Christ, to which you were also called in one body, rule your hearts. And be thankful."
>
> —Colossians 3:13-15 CSB

The truth is, when we forgive, we're doing ourselves an incredible favor. When we decide to forgive and pray for God to bless our enemies and love them like Jesus loves them, God is faithful and He will change our hearts as we keep doing what's right according to His Word.

> *Lord, soften my heart to be like Yours and Your Son's. Help me to warm up to You by being in Your presence. And in that warmth, mold me with Your hands until I'm covered with the fingerprints of forgiveness.*

Michael is responsible for putting these collections together and produces books through Story Builds Creative (Story-Builds.com). He helps Christian writers get their life-changing words into the world on a budget! Get your free writing resource guide at DevoWriters.com to get started!

Michael writes fiction under the pen name M. Lacey. Get some of his stories and books at fiction.michaellacey.me. Coming from the rich writing heritage of Mississippi, he believes in the power of words to inspire and encourage. It is a lifelong calling to put pen to paper (or fingertips to keys) for him, and he doesn't take it lightly.

Finally, Michael is a singer/songwriter and worship leader who is always looking to collaborate and co-write. Find out more (and get some free music) at michaellaceymusic.com.

His goal is to spend as much time with his family as possible, especially while his children are young. Jobs and money come and go, but time only passes. If you'd like to support him in any way, reach out or join his mailing lists to get all of his newest content.

michaellacey.me | Story-Builds.com | DevoWriters.com
Devotional Author Profile: https://amzn.to/3iGe5AO
Fiction Author Profile: https://amzn.to/30dupdg

TWO

Should We Forgive God?

MICHAEL LACEY

"For I consider that the sufferings of this present time are not worth comparing with the glory that is going to be revealed to us."

—Romans 8:18 (CSB)

Over the last several years, I feel I've been obedient to God in my career choices, but no matter what I do, we don't seem to make a lot of progress. I've encountered more failure than success, financially, and I struggle with knowing whether or not I've really been obedient or if God just has a bigger plan. The thought crossed my mind that maybe I've been offended by God. Of course, I pushed that away as soon as it came because I know He is good and wants good for us. The problem is that I define 'good' differently than He does, and that can be frustrating! However, I know what it's like to know that God let difficult things happen to you.

So, do you ever feel you need to forgive God? What an arrogant thought, yet it's not too crazy to think that we may have been hurt by Him. The truth is not that He has hurt us but that we have seen His actions and allowances as hurt from Him. Is it possible you were wrong about the situation? If that's the case, is it possible you are wrong about other grievances because you have a more limited view of everything that is happening?

For me, I was defining what my life should look like now rather than what God is molding it into for my good and His glory.

Or maybe the thing that hurt you wasn't meant to hurt you. In today's culture, it's easy to crank up our sensitivities. It's possible you allowed yourself to be too frazzled or even unguarded, and the action resulted in pain. Are we then too sensitive? Are we a bunch of "Karen's" running around looking for ways to be offended? No, that's not what I'm saying, though it's certainly possible for each of us! My point is that when we feel hurt by something God allowed, we must trust that He has bigger plans, sometimes for us and sometimes for others.

It would be arrogant to stare defiantly at the Maker of the universe and tell Him He did something wrong:

"You shouldn't have let that happen. Do know how painful it is? Why would You put me through that?"

Why, indeed? God is holding you in His righteous right hand, and Romans 8 reminds us that His actions come from love, whether it's some kind of consequence, protection, or even proving His right to glory, He is good and worthy of our obedience, honor, and trust.

Consider letting these offenses go not as allowance for the weakness of others but in reverence of the sovereignty of God. If He let it happen, He has a reason. Let's not fight against Him or push the lesson and potential growth further away, let's lean in closer to Him each time we are hurt. Let us say to Him,

> *Dad, this hurts, and I know You know that. Show me what you want me to learn or do. Help me to trust Your hand with this, and if it's Your will, take it away. If not, help me to still give You glory through it.*

THREE

The Hardest Person to Forgive

MICHAEL LACEY

"Then Peter approached him and asked, "Lord, how many times must I forgive my brother or sister who sins against me? As many as seven times?"

"I tell you, not as many as seven," Jesus replied, "but seventy times seven.""

—Matthew 18:21-22 (CSB)

I'm sorry, I just can't forgive you. If only you didn't keep doing the same thing over and over again, hurting me and limiting my potential because of your inadequacies. I forgave you the first couple of times, but this is like #489. If there was a way to get away from you, I probably would.

This is a conversation I've had to have several times in my heart but never aloud. Who do you suppose that person is? My spouse? A sibling? A parent or child? Who is it for you? While there are people who may warrant such a rebuke, this is a snapshot of me talking to...myself.

The Favor of Forgiveness

For me, wasting time is one of my biggest sins, and God is teaching me a lot about what redeeming the time actually means in my life. I'm easily distracted and pulled to various other tasks when I'm trying to accomplish something specific. So, the work-day sprints by, and it's time to pick up the kids before I've really made progress as hoped. And who suffers for it? My family. They get a frustrated version of me when I don't live up to my potential in the day. And that happens more often than I'd like.

But who am I to talk down to any of God's creation, much less the one I know best? Yet, I often chide myself for falling short on a daily, if not hourly, basis. But the word says so much about this. One teaching is to love yourself as you love your neighbor. Well, other verses talk about forgiving your 'neighbors' over and over again. In fact, one verse suggests 70x7 times. I used to think that meant 490 offenses per person, but I recently learned that the verse might mean 490 times PER offense. It doesn't give a number of overall offenses. Regardless, the consensus among commentaries here is that the actual number isn't important, the concept is to continually forgive. So if that's all true for my neighbor, it's true for the way we should forgive ourselves. After all, God has released us from our bounds, so why put them back on?

> "As far as the east is from the west, so far has he removed our transgressions from us."
>
> —Psalms 103:12 CSB

You, Christ-follower*, are forgiven. This is such a powerful reminder. I still have a hard time believing that He forgives and knows our sin no more. I will continue to recite that scripture over me when I hear the lies of the enemy saying, "you'll never outrun your mistakes." I will choose to listen to the voice of truth.

God, help me to strive to live to the standards You've placed on my life and throughout Your word, but also give me grace to extend to myself when I fall short. Use it to remind me of my great need for You as well as the great responsibility of forgiving others.

*If you don't know Christ, He still knows you and wants *you* to know Him. He knows you because His Father knit you together in your mother's womb. There are salvation prayers, but it is not the words that save you; it's the power of Christ as you surrender your will to Him, trusting that He is who He says He is, the Word of God is true, and the Lord and Savior of your life. The words don't have to be spoken if you believe in your heart, but you will one day have to make it known before men, confessing the name of Jesus unashamedly. Experience His unconditional love, His peace that goes beyond all understanding, hope that does not disappoint, and joy indescribable. Walk in freedom, starting now.

FOUR

Forgive Before Offense

MICHAEL LACEY

"How shall they believe in him whom they have not heard?"

—Romans 10:14

Often offense comes from a place of pride. When someone cuts me off in traffic or skips lanes, it's possible they aren't aware of the law. I know, that one's a stretch. How about when someone steals something? To many of us, we know why stealing is wrong and how it offends our God, but some have been taught that taking some things is acceptable because the only one hurt is the larger organization who won't 'miss' it anyways.

I see people post online or say things that hurt my heart, but not just for the thing being said. What I've learned is those people are speaking and acting out of pain. Something in them has been offended, mistreated, or misinformed, and their response comes from a distorted view of life and its purposes. I'm not saying they are always wrong, but I've started to have compassion for them. Rather than being offended by their stance, I choose to pray for them while also asking God why I might be offended before I let it get too far.

We all have different backgrounds. You don't know what someone's home-life and influences did to them to create distorted mindsets and leanings. They are hurting, and sometimes pain is all they know, both in giving and receiving, whether they're aware or not. People respond in certain ways because they haven't had a guiding light, a wise teacher, or a biblical example in their lives. How can we expect someone to follow a rule they don't know exists or to live to a standard they've never heard of?

And if that's true, how much am I lacking? What hurts are clouding my views and insights? While not always successful, I try to gauge some situations before they have a chance to get to me. Another phrase for that is 'extending grace' before offense can set in. The truth is, we've all had a rough life or difficult experiences, and many have had it even worse.

They don't need to be 'put in their place'; sometime we need to be 'put in their place' so we can grow in compassion. If our response is mercy, then grace on top of that, imagine what their response might be. God pours out mercy first by not giving us what we deserve, then grace by giving more than we deserve. In that case, what is your response?

People need grace more than you need justification. They need the love of God flowing through you more than they need another person thinking they are trash. They need a glimpse of Jesus in a lifetime of seeing hypocrisy in Christianity. In approaching people with love and extending grace in advance, we can offset offense, push away pain, and forgive before we're affronted. And more than that, we can break chains through the power of the Holy Spirit moving through us as others are surprised by grace.

> "The best time to forgive is before we are ever offended. The next best time to forgive is right now."
> —Lysa TerKeurst, *Forgiving What You Can't Forget*

God, help me to see people the way You see them. Help me to understand that they, like me, are walking through a field of fractured hurts, struggling to navigate emotionally debris in the darkness. Help me to be a light to them as I reflect Your goodness, mercy, kindness, and grace.

FIVE

For the Saving of Many

MICHAEL LACEY

> "You intended to harm me, but God intended it for good to accomplish what is now being done, the saving of many lives."
>
> —Genesis 50:20 (NIV)

Many of us know the story of Joseph and how God used the terrible things in his life to put him in place to save many people. It's one of my favorite accounts and puts Joseph to the top of my list of Bible heroes. It's an incredible story, but we often overlook a few details, specifically in the realm of forgiveness. Read through the account here:

> "When Joseph's brothers saw that their father was dead, they said, "What if Joseph holds a grudge against us and pays us back for all the wrongs we did to him?" So they sent word to Joseph, saying, "Your father left these instructions before he died: 'This is what you are to say to Joseph: I ask you to forgive

your brothers the sins and the wrongs they committed in treating you so badly.' Now please forgive the sins of the servants of the God of your father." When their message came to him, Joseph wept. His brothers then came and threw themselves down before him. "We are your slaves," they said. But Joseph said to them, "Don't be afraid. Am I in the place of God?" —Genesis 50:15-19 (NIV)

Look at this progression of events, and consider all the perspectives and possibilities:

- Joseph was treated well by his *father*, then sold by his brothers.
- Later in life, he has power, their fate in his hands.
- His *father*—who always treated him well—asked him to forgive the brothers. His father didn't ask for Joseph to save the family, just to forgive them.
- Then, Joseph wept. He mourned so much loss: his father and their relationship that he could have had, the family ties that were broken, the pain he suffered, maybe even the pain and hunger his family was going through.
- It doesn't say how long he wept, but the progression moves quickly enough to assume he didn't stay in that posture long.
- His brothers, being forgiven (whether they knew it or not), laid themselves at his feet, offering themselves as slaves to him.
- Joseph told them not to be afraid. He provided for all of them and their children. He didn't just forgive them, he understood that God

allowed all of this "for the saving of many lives."

So, did Joseph have a righteous indignation after this? Did he say or think, "that's right, look at me know?" Did he hold the grudge? Nope, he truly forgave them. He forgave them of an action that changed his *entire* life. And out of that, his perspective shifted right away. After he said he would provide for them, verse 21 says, **"he reassured them and spoke kindly to them."**

> *"We must develop and maintain the capacity to forgive. He who is devoid of the power to forgive is devoid of the power to love... Forgiveness does not mean ignoring what has been done or putting a false label on an evil act. It means, rather, that the evil act no longer remains as a barrier to the relationship. Forgiveness is a catalyst creating the atmosphere necessary for a fresh start and a new beginning." — Martin Luther King Jr. in a sermon published in A Gift of Love.*

Father, I know You've always treated me well even when others haven't. And I know You're asking me to forgive so that You can do something amazing through it. Give me the wisdom to weep, the moment to mourn, and the resilience to release. I trust You.

SIX

The Prison

AMI LOPER

> "Beloved, never avenge yourselves, but leave it to the wrath of God, for it is written, 'Vengeance is mine, I will repay, says the Lord.'"
>
> —Romans 12:19

His single clap bounced off the block walls and around the large, nearly empty church as he described the sound of iron bars slamming shut behind him.

But this man was no prisoner; he was a warden at the state penitentiary. His words as he described his experience of going to work each day would echo in my head for weeks and I didn't understand why.

"When I go to work, those bars slam shut behind me," he told our small group of early morning pray-ers with one enormous clap resounding in my ears and in my heart. "I'm as much a prisoner as the prisoners."

No one else probably thought a thing about it; he was simply describing his job. But the Holy Spirit brought me back and back to those words like a persistent tapping on my shoulder until I understood what He wanted me to hear.

I was a warden too.

I hadn't done the crime, but I wanted to make sure my abuser paid for his and now my heart felt imprisoned, trapped in the fortress I had formed with my unforgiveness. My prisoner wasn't free to go, but neither was I. I had to stay there, surrounded by those cold prison walls to make sure he paid the debt he owed.

Little did I realize that by maintaining the debt, I maintained a connection to him. Though being as far from him as possible in location was all I wanted, my unforgiveness kept me chained to him in ways I couldn't see.

We serve a God who loves justice. He makes it clear in His Word that bringing people to justice is part of His character as He defends the oppressed. I loved this about my Jesus; He fought for me when I was weak. He came to my rescue and extracted me from a life of painful and heartbreaking abuse. My desire for justice wasn't sin. Yet my desire to implement justice myself was more than the human heart was designed to carry. It would destroy me if I didn't let it go.

In my mind, I could see myself wasting my days as the warden of this one who had already stolen enough of my life. Was the debt owed me worth so much that I would waste even one more day to see it paid? Could it really ever be paid? Could I trust God enough to hand the keys over to Him?

I sat in a folding chair alone in my room staring teary-eyed at the empty folding chair I had set up adjacent to me. The words came slow and measured. I wanted to do this completely.

"I forgive you," came the trembling whisper as I imagined my abuser in the empty chair. "I cancel the debt," I said with determination as the tears flowed down. "I release you," came the guttural cry as I felt the pain of surrender that brought me freedom.

> *Lord, examine my heart. Are there still places I'm holding onto the debt someone owes me? Are there any ways in which I've set myself up as the warden in a feeble attempt to procure justice on my own? I want to live in the freedom you died to give me. I'm weary from my need for justice taking precedence over my need for freedom. My heart wasn't made to execute justice over the life of those who have hurt me. I surrender that role to You. I trust You to defend me.*

Ami has been preaching since her teens and has her Master's Degree in Theology. A gleeful puzzler, a persistent solution-finder, a hunter of clarity, Ami finds her joy in discovering connections and truths tucked in corners of the Word of God.

As an author and a guest speaker in churches and conferences, she brings those truths to light as she crafts words that bring transformation. Ami's mission is to use the challenges she's been through to resource others into their freedom by bringing hope to the wounded, spiritual food to the hungry, tools to the learning, and kinship for the invisible.

Ami and her husband live in Arizona and love few things more than surrounding themselves with their children and their growing number of grandchildren.

Connect with Ami on her website, amiloper.com, and on the socials, where you can find her by name.

SEVEN

The Gift of Grief

AMI LOPER

> "For godly grief produces a repentance that leads to salvation without regret, whereas worldly grief produces death."
>
> —2 Corinthians 7:10

I had given my life back to the Lord. Why didn't I feel completely better?

Taking my life in my hands had broken me. I had run headlong from the hand of God into the hands of verbal and physical abuse. Thinking I would find love, I found pain. Each day seemed to bring new and inventive ways for me to be abused, to feel small, helpless, unloved and used.

But I had run home. I had given my life back to God and He had graciously provided a way of escape from the hellish life in which I had found myself. I was starting over, rebuilding the broken pieces. The physical signs of abuse had begun to fade, and I had found a measure of confidence in finally saying enough is enough.

Yet the feeling of a stone in my gut persisted. It went with me everywhere, whether I was playing with my baby girl or laying in bed alone each night.

The Lord was never gentler to me than He was during that time. I see it now as I look back. He never, in compassionless tyranny, demanded that I forgive; instead, He allowed me to grow in absolute hatred for the wasting disease of unforgiveness.

Unforgiveness was the cause of my nightmares, of my simmering anger, of my deep valley of depression. Unforgiveness was the stone in my stomach.

In turning back to the Lord, I sought His forgiveness with tears. I washed His feet countless times in those tears. Yet, like the layers of an onion, healing only *began* with seeking forgiveness. A layer of grief would come before we got to the core of my need to forgive.

Before I could forgive, I needed to grieve.

There was grace to grieve. I'd had such grand, albeit foolish, hopes for my wayward attempts to find love. I had made a covenant before God that I grieved had been broken by another's lack of love, fidelity, and care. I had lost my ability to trust and my innocence in so many ways. I had brought a precious and blameless child into the chaos that was partly my own creation. My life felt over though I was still in my teens. I grieved.

It was right to grieve. And I believe that God grieved with me even as He guided me through my grief. If I hadn't grieved, I wouldn't have comprehended the full spectrum of ramifications of the sin committed against me. And if I couldn't look that sin squarely in the face and name it, how could I forgive it with the completeness that washed away not only the sin, but the stain of the sin from my life?

Grief gave me the gift of clarity. In my grieving I clearly saw my own sin, my own blame in my imploded life. In my grieving I clearly saw the events and heart attitudes that had led me to run from God. In my grief I saw the ugliness of sin and the beauty of the forgiveness I had received. My grief brought me from the repentance that said, "Oh Lord, I'm sorry for what my life has become" to the repentance that said, "Oh Lord, forgive me for what I have done."

> *Lord, I am grieving all that has been lost and stolen in my life. I grieve for the losses I have caused and for the losses caused by the sin of others. Carry me, Lord, through this grief. I don't want to get stuck in grief, but I want to fully grieve so that I can fully surrender these losses to You and trust You to redeem them. I pray for the gift of clarity that grief can bring so that I can see the past clearly and then put it behind me as I reach toward the good and hope-filled future You have for me.*

EIGHT

Gila Monster Attack

AMI LOPER

"But one thing I do: forgetting what lies behind and straining forward to what lies ahead, I press on toward the goal for the prize of the upward call of God in Christ Jesus."

—Philippians 3:13-14

I grew up in southern Arizona, between Tucson and the border of Mexico. Interesting thing about growing up in the middle of nowhere: school assemblies are... different. Instead of talking about the safety concerns of crossing the street, they discuss the safety concerns of getting lost in the desert. I learned which cactus to eat if I was thirsty, how to listen for a rattlesnake and some interesting things about Gila monsters.

Gila monsters aren't that big, but they are ferocious. If one attacks and bites you, their jaws lock and they *cannot* let go. At age eight, I was told the best way to get one off. I'll spare you the details, but it involves a machete. I don't know about all the other eight-year-olds, but this little, prissy thing didn't carry a machete. Where was I going to keep it? In my lace-fringed socks?

Without the machete, the only way to get the Gila monster off you is simply to rip it off. Yeah, it'll hurt pretty bad, and you may die from blood loss, but it's the only way. (Eight-year-old nightmares, commence.)

Then about a decade ago, I got attacked, not by a Gila monster, but by someone I thought I could trust. Someone who maligned me and turned those closest to me against me. I flashed back to those horrifying Gila monsters as I felt the teeth of betrayal sink into me.

As I sought the Lord on how to detach this thing from me so I could halt the blood loss and keep it from killing me, He graciously guided me.

First, the Lord encouraged me to not deny reality. A Gila monster really did attack. It's nothing to be ashamed of. It happened; that's life.

Second, yank it off. With shocking frequency, I found myself caressing my Gila monster instead of getting rid of it. I found myself rehearsing the pain instead of rehearsing how God had carried me through the pain. We all have a choice: keep your monster and die or tear it off and live.

Third, I needed to get care. I am so blessed by my husband and my true friends who helped to bandage my wounds and purge out the poisons. They have been a crucial part of the healing process. As I expressed the pain in my heart while reminding myself of God's faithfulness, I moved forward.

Fourth, walk in wholeness. This is not really a step in the process; it is the essential element amid all the previous steps. Get in the Presence of God and let Him speak truth to you. Be willing to be healed by His love. Without healing time in God's Presence woven throughout the entire process, these steps could easily turn into denial or perpetual whining. But with God working with you in the process, you'll be placing yourself in a position for growth, maturity and healing.

> *Lord, this unwarranted attack has completely blindsided me and I am stunned and in pain. Please give me Your perspective of what I'm walking through right now so that I can begin to see hope emerge beyond this ache. As I forgive, help me to also leave this chapter of my story behind, to not rehearse it or camp out in this painful place. Bring wise and godly counselors into my life with whom I can process and who will speak healing into my wounds. I want to walk in wholeness, Lord. I trust You to heal my heart.*

NINE

How Do You Spell Relief?

JACKIE PERSEGHETTI

> While a 1970's commercial introduced the concept of spelling relief as R-O-L-A-I-D-S,
>
> Jesus introduced the concept centuries before by spelling it as F-O-R-G-I-V-E-N.

I don't know about you, but the acidity of life sometimes eats away at my insides. This has been especially true this year while dealing with the frustrations of Covid, observing the actions of others I may disagree with, and filtering through mixed messages on social media, watching relationships implode.

While some may spell relief with an antacid, others may spell relief by reaching for a distraction, or a pleasure, or all of the above. But those forms of relief are ineffective and need constant feeding to keep the symptoms at bay. Jesus didn't come to deal with the symptoms we face in life, but rather the root causes. In James 1:14 we learn that our passions are often driven by selfish desires which lead us down a deadly path.

In Jeremiah 17:9 we are reminded that our heart is so deceitful and desperately sick, no one can understand it. But, in all that darkness, God offers us relief and hope. Romans 5:8 addresses the fact that when we were worthless, and offensive, Jesus sacrificed His life to reclaim us. And then because of Jesus' sacrifice we get to walk in places of new freedom (see Romans 8:1-2)!

Only God's way of spelling relief has been proven the most effective when tested. Here is what His relief offers for those who turn to Jesus to be forgiven:

F -- Fellowship with God and the joy of being fully known -- yet loved -- by Him

O -- Optimism and hope because Jesus knows our frailties and invites us to lean on His strength

R -- Release from having to perform. Our life changes from a life of *shoulds* to a life of *get-tos*

G -- Gifts God equips us with to do the good work He's prepared for us to walk into

I -- Identity as a child of God having been adopted into His family and sharing in Jesus' inheritance

V -- Victory and release from being enslaved to sin and self because of Jesus' sacrifice on our behalf

E -- Encouragement and growth as God's Holy Spirit teaches us and makes His Word come alive

N -- Newness of Life and restoration of our soul as God grows us to be more like Jesus

Be encouraged! Jesus offers us so much more than anything we may reach for in the heartburn of life. Relief spelled God's way is true relief!

Lord, how often I'm tempted to reach for distraction or pleasure instead of all that you've provided for me as Your child -- fully forgiven, and fully provided for. Please help me to... (finish the prayer in your own words)

Jackie Perseghetti wants to live in a world that is no longer broken and God's presence is known and enjoyed. As a best-selling author of four devotional books, Jackie is passionate about helping others cultivate an undivided heart so they can walk in new places of simplicity, freedom, and authenticity with the Lord.

When she's not writing or teaching, you can find her encouraging others over coffee, strolling with her husband and their two rescue dogs, abruptly stopping to capture nature with her cell phone, and loving on her grandkids.

You can find Jackie at www.AKingdomHeartbeat.com and on Instagram and Pinterest.

TEN

The Art of Asking Forgiveness

JACKIE PERSEGHETTI

> Therefore, as God's chosen people, holy and dearly loved, clothe yourselves with compassion, kindness, humility, gentleness and patience.
>
> –Colossians 3:12 (NIV)

It happened so quickly. In a moment of frustration, my words reached across the counter and slapped the stranger standing behind it across his face (metaphorically). He had been unyielding, uncaring, and matter-of-fact as he flatly stated I couldn't take any form of bag down into the cave. Even though I explained I knew the rules and had called in advance and was granted permission because of medical necessity, he was unimpressed. He was there to follow the black-and-white lettering on the sign with no regard for any prior arrangements that had been made. Either I go underground for two hours without my emergency supplies, or we turn around and drive the three hours home.

Like Gandolf against the Balrag, he stood his ground with a determined, "You shall not pass!" Well, where my feet couldn't traverse, my words certainly could. "Look," I challenged, "Even with this bag slung across my body, I'm still smaller than a fat person." As soon as those words left my mouth, I saw a flicker of pain in his eyes. I hadn't given thought to his large, heavyweight stature. And the Holy Spirit convicted my heart. With a defeated expression, he handed me my ticket. I had won the argument and gotten what I wanted -- but at what cost?

Clothe yourself with *compassion* -- compassion acknowledges the unseen story of another and doesn't belittle or dismiss. *Kindness* acknowledges the dignity of someone and doesn't demand perfection. *Humility* acknowledges the fact we are *all* walking wounded, in need of a Savior. *Gentleness* and *patience* acknowledge the hard work of loving others as the Lord has chosen to love us.

Having taken several steps away, I did a prompt u-turn and approached the attendant to ask his forgiveness. The pain in his eyes swelled into tears. I was the first person in his life to ask him for forgiveness, and he wasn't sure how to respond. While we may often say, "I'm sorry," we aren't necessarily asking for forgiveness. Asking for forgiveness is just that -- asking for forgiveness. Here is an example of what that can look like:

I would like to ask your forgiveness for (name the offense / the specific action you did). *It was* (acknowledge the offense for what it was: rude, disrespectful, unkind, selfish, etc.) *Do you forgive me?* (and wait for a response.

If they wave it off with, "no problem," reply with, *thank you, but do you forgive me?* and then wait for their response and journey where the conversation may lead from there.)

This is how I asked the attendant's forgiveness, and I watched the burden of pain roll off his shoulders -- and mine as well. We had a nice chat afterwards. Although I had royally messed up, God used that whole scenario in his life, mine, and even those who had been onlooking.

The art of asking forgiveness can be learned and practiced to keep it from becoming a lost art. Think about someone you recently offended. Using the example above, complete the blanks for how you could ask their forgiveness. If you make a point to practice this art (in real life), don't be surprised to see doors open and hearts soften -- including yours!

ELEVEN

Past Pretending

JACKIE PERSEGHETTI

"Forgiveness is the fragrance that the violet sheds on the heel that has crushed it."

—Mark Twain

It had been 30 years since our last interaction -- an interaction that knocked the wind out of me, beat me like a punching bag, and left me crumpled on the floor. Her eyes were full of judgement, her tongue an emotional shredder, and she had a demanding and cutting demeanor. She made me stagger as if in a boxing ring, just before going down from a final knockout punch that came out of the blue. And this was just a normal interaction, not even a fighting match. Encounters with this person often inflicted deep wounds and emotional bruises. And if I never had to see her again, it would be too soon!

But 30 years later, there she was...in the pew right in front of me at our Christmas Eve service at church. Apparently, she was visiting.

My heart pounded and stomach soured as I wrestled with memories of the past. I was battling two unwelcomed visitors -- the one sitting before me, and wounds brought to the surface. I could pretend I didn't see her and look the other way, I plotted, or pretend I didn't recognize her if she noticed me. I could even pretend she may have changed. But that would be pretending -- both about the past and the present.

So. There I sat, with a choice looming over my head that squeezed my heart into a rapid, pounding pulse. Although it's been said, *"Forgiveness is the fragrance the violet sheds on the heel that has crushed it,"* I feared being crushed, and I wanted the crusher to understand the hurt she inflicts.

During the service, my mind moved past the baby in the manger, to Jesus paraded through the streets along with two thieves -- the innocent with the guilty in an association of shame. Prior to that event, Jesus was blindfolded, spat upon, slapped, and taunted as his persecutors sarcastically egged Him on to guess who struck Him. Then He endured a brutal whipping where pieces of His flesh were ripped from His back, and a crown of jagged thorns shoved onto His head. All of this assault came on the heels of having already been betrayed, denied, and abandoned--and just prior to being publicly humiliated, shamed, and crushed.

Yet, Jesus forgave them all. As He hung on the cross, He also asked the Father to forgive them as well. Jesus didn't pretend there were no offenses. He didn't pretend it didn't hurt. He knew. And He forgave. So. There I sat with both His example and a choice before me. It was time to move past pretending.

Acknowledging the hurt, I offered it to the Lord as a gift. (Yes. He wants all of us -- even the ugly, broken, angry, bitter, hurtful, wounded, helpless and hopeless portions!) When the service ended, I gently tapped her on the back. She turned around, our eyes met, and God surprised me with the love He poured into my heart towards her. It was an unexpected, healing moment.

Oh Lord, You know how hard it is for me to let go of (name what you're holding onto) Please remove any fear, anger, or desire to punish (name of person) for the hurt they've inflicted. Lord, You know ...

TWELVE

The (Un)chosen Yoke

JACKIE PERSEGHETTI

> Come to me all who labor and are heavy laden, and I will give you rest. Take my yoke upon you, and learn from me, for I am gentle and lowly in heart, and you will find rest for your souls. For my yoke is easy, and my burden is light.
>
> —Matthew 28-30 (ESV)

Shame. Rejection. Fear. Defeat. Isolation. Have you ever been under the yoke of unforgiveness? I have. It's a merciless taskmaster that straddles our shoulders and drives our emotions and actions. Sometimes it's thrust upon our backs from others withholding their forgiveness toward us. Sometimes it falls upon us like a heavy weight when we choose to withhold forgiveness toward them. But there is yet another yoke of unforgiveness -- a yoke that is silent, overlooked, and deadly. It is the yoke of me not forgiving myself.

When I silently choose this yoke, I lie to myself that I'm in control. I feel if I wear it long enough it will change me into a better person -- one who will never do/say/feel *that* again. Plowing through life with this yoke strapped to my back will help me not offend, hurt, or disappoint others. And if I plow hard enough, maybe the whole mess I made will be paid for, and I'll finally be able to live with myself. Or so the lie goes. But that's not walking in the forgiveness Jesus offers me.

When I want to run and hide due to shame, Jesus says come. He invites me in the midst of watching me toil under that heavy yoke. He doesn't give me more work or fields to plow in punishment; He gives me rest. I love a picture I once saw of an ancient yoke. It had two differently sized neck harnesses -- one big, and one small. When a young ox was being trained to plow, it would be paired with a mature ox. The bigger animal did all the work and pulled all the weight. The younger one had to merely learn to walk alongside. Do you see a beautiful word picture here?

Jesus says His yoke is easy, and His burden is light. In fact, Jesus mentions the idea of rest not just once, but twice. Twice! Where our yoke of not forgiving ourselves results in shame, His yoke results in freedom. Where our yoke is worn through rejection, His yoke is worn through invitation. Where our yoke produces fear, His yoke produces security. Where our yoke provides defeat, His yoke provides strength. And where our yoke drives us to isolation, His yoke drives us to Himself.

Jesus goes beyond the mere granting of forgiveness. He woos us back to Himself where He takes the responsibility of doing all the heavy lifting. Our first step in the journey is choosing His yoke over our own, and accepting His invitation to walk beside Him.

Oh Lord, my heart is tired and weary. I've worked under a yoke of unforgiveness for so long, I'm not sure I know how to rest. Can you please teach me? I want to choose Your yoke. Please free me from this yoke of . . .

THIRTEEN

When I Hide My Sin

MIRANDA J. CHIVERS

> When I kept silent, my bones wasted away through my groaning all day long. For day and night your hand was heavy on me; my strength was sapped as in the heat of summer. Then I acknowledged my sin to you and did not cover up my iniquity. I said, "I will confess my transgressions to the Lord. And you forgave the guilt of my sin.
>
> —Psalm 32: 3-5 (NIV)

Is there an unconfessed sin that's "wasting your bones"? Are shame and guilt sabotaging your confession and destroying your well-being? The Bible says repentance is essential to experiencing forgiveness.

In this passage from Psalms, King David says that his sin of adultery with Bathsheba caused his bones to "waste away" and sap his strength. This picture of prolonged guilt shows chronic depression with the added symptoms of weight loss, low energy, and extreme sadness. It demonstrates how the covering up of sin impairs our physical and mental health.

Perhaps your sin isn't adultery, like King David confesses here. Maybe it's as small as telling a little white lie or keeping the extra change from the rattled store clerk; or not leaving a note on that car you scuffed when you opened the car door. But later, you discover that your mistake had profound consequences for another. And then....

Admitting that we've sinned is humiliating. What will people think of us?

We dismiss the importance of confession, even though we know it's good for the soul. If no one knows about the sin, then who are we hurting? Is it really that important?

It's natural to ignore, excuse, rationalize, justify, or blame another when we mess up. We fear the discovery of these sins by others, so we push them into the secret spaces of our heart. By pushing away our guilt, we try to make ourselves look better than we really are. But the result is costly.

These hidden sins fester and niggle at our consciences, reminding us of our imperfections. When they pile up, our mental health suffers. We become sad and discouraged. Our speech and attitude turn negative. Our self-worth nosedives and our relationships fail.

When shame and guilt eat away at our souls, the bad we've done doesn't go away just because we wish it to do so. There's always a price to be paid for sin.

The Favor of Forgiveness

God wants us to succeed in life and to have good self-esteem so we can serve him and others. Success starts with a pure heart. This leads to positive attitudes, clean speech and compassionate responses. Then we can experience guilt-free and blame-free relationships without barriers; and enjoy the freedom of healthy boundaries, and honest, open communication.

Doctors recognize the need for confession and forgiveness to encourage mental and physical healing. They name it therapy. In Christianity, it's called repentance. Confessing our shortcomings releases the guilt that keeps us bound and frees us from shame.

When King David repented, God forgave. The guilt left and he was restored.

Restoring our self-esteem and our relationships requires that we come out of hiding and speak the truth about our sin. Through humble confession, we too can be healed.

Jesus died to set us free. Let us then be free indeed.

> *Jesus, I humbly confess my sins. I repent of (offense) and hurting (person offended). I now recognize that I hurt myself by hiding from my sin. Lord, I know I hurt you most of all. I confess this all to you now. Forgive me. Take away my guilt and shame and make me whole. In Jesus' name.*

Miranda J. Chivers is the author of "Unequally Yoked: Staying Committed to Jesus and Your Unbelieving Spouse," and ministers to an unequally yoked marriage support group on Facebook. Purchase the book on Amazon and join the support group on Facebook.

Miranda J. Chivers (a.k.a. MJ Krause-Chivers) fiction series portrays the cultural genocide of the Russian Mennonite people in southern Ukraine during the Russian Revolution and explores the challenges in recovering from inter-generational trauma. Russian Mennonite Chronicles: Book One: Katarina's Dark Shadow is available on Amazon.

Amazon.com/author/mirandajchivers

FOURTEEN

When Nations Sin

MIRANDA J. CHIVERS

"For judgment is without mercy to one who has shown no mercy. Mercy triumphs over judgment."

—James 2:13

Forgiveness and mercy are imperative to resolving conflict. Both are necessary in repairing relationships and righting wrongs. But on both a personal and global level, these tasks are rarely easy.

When we repent, we expect God to forgive us. But when it's our turn to be merciful, holding grudges often comes easier than following Christ's example. Sadly, some relationships are not restorable despite forgiveness. The hurt is too deep or the crime too intimate. And when death happens, it's the surviving family and/or the broader community that struggles to forgive. Or conversely, to repent.

National sins are one example.

In the spring of 2021, the world held their breath when researchers discovered the unmarked graves of over one thousand First Nations children at three former residential schools in Canada — the evidence of a forced assimilation experiment gone terribly wrong. As I write this, the search for more bodies continues.

As a Canadian, I collectively share with my government the guilt and shame of perpetuating ethnic cleansing against a people whose only crime was being different. The pain of separation and alienation felt by those families and communities during the decades of that dreadful policy, has resurfaced with this discovery; and the challenging emotional work of healing to find closure is ongoing.

Today, I ask the First Nations peoples for forgiveness and beg for mercy.

In the middle of this breaking news and halfway around the globe, Ukraine unveils a monument and apologizes for the cultural genocide against my Mennonite ancestors during and following the Russian revolution. Smashed markers from razed graves that are now being resurrected and repaired are chilling reminders of the murders, the theft of our homes and our expulsion from the country. Ukraine seeks my forgiveness.

I am angry at the intergenerational trauma caused by those government policies against my people one hundred years ago. This also compels me to consider the comparable suffering experienced by the First Nations peoples today.

Neither case involved me by name. Yet, in Canada, I bear the shame of being a partner in crime. In Ukraine,

The Favor of Forgiveness

I am the victims' family. This is a strange and surreal moment and I struggle to describe my feelings.

Genocide, as a by-product of war, has crushed cultures and families since Cain killed Abel. Overpowering the weaker reflects our need to feed our egos and make ourselves feel superior. Our natural tendency is the desire to be God-like — dictating global rules and dominating the less powerful. But history has proven the destructiveness of this behavior.

As first world nations, we are slow to learn the necessity of caution in governing. There are consequences when we violate human rights. We cannot cover up these sins indefinitely. Judgement will come. The world is watching.

As Christians, we are charged with the tasks of mediating conflict, encouraging peace and unity, and embracing forgiveness and mercy. We must lead by example and be the light shining in the darkness — not only on a personal level but also globally. The past serves as a reminder to guard our actions today. We can lead our nations to righteousness and work together to bring the Kingdom of Heaven to earth. We are the only Jesus the world sees.

> *Heavenly Father, forgive us for our sins against humanity. Make us ever mindful of our words and actions and teach us to love others the way you love us — unconditionally and without reservation. Help us heal the hurts and point the world to you.*

FIFTEEN

Forgiving Myself

MIRANDA J. CHIVERS

"Remember not the former things, nor consider the things of old. Behold, I am doing a new thing; now it springs forth, do you not perceive it? I will make a way in the wilderness and rivers in the desert."

—Isaiah 43:18-19

When a parent's life ends, a strange void fills the space once held by their presence. Then, a plethora of feelings surround the cherished memories. We mourn missed opportunities, words said or not, and fractured relationships.

As my mother's time neared, I reflected on our rocky bond. I'd always wanted the Hollywood image of the perfect mother-daughter rapport—shopping together, reading the same books, or just girl-talking over a cup of tea. But it was never to be. Other than sharing recipes and gardening tips, we had little connection. I felt cheated by the unresolved push-pull dynamic that defined our union.

My 'aha moment' came at the end. Although too late to be helpful, it soothed this deep wound. Ever the exuberant extrovert, mom's personality clashed with my introverted self. If only we'd both acknowledged this sooner.

Dad understood me better than mom. With similar personalities and a united love of the written word, we connected more deeply as he aged. Since we lived too far apart to enjoy walks in the countryside or picnics at the lake, I looked forward to our Sunday night phone calls. But some things could not be shared. I hid the pain of my traumas and mental illness, and pretended that all was well. At his deathbed, I regretted the missed years caused by simple misunderstandings and anger at my mother. Then, it was too late to undo my lack of honesty, or replace the lost days, or repent for the pain I'd caused. There was nothing I could take back.

Everyone experiences hurt. And regrets come from careless words, rude actions or unmet expectations. Each morning brings a reminder of yesterday's mistakes. Destructive words hang in the air and relationships dissolve. But it's unhelpful to dwell on things we cannot change.

Thankfully, God redeems us. In those dark places lie lessons for our future. When we repent, He enriches our lives by reshaping us for his glory. Our ashes are God's beauty. Through failure and loss, we gain the tools of compassion and valuable insight that enable us to encourage others. Forgiving ourselves requires learning from our regrets and stepping into freedom. Isaiah 43:18-19 tells us to forget the past and press forward.

God is doing a new thing in our lives. He wants to rewrite our ugly yesterdays and turn them into beautiful tomorrows. Are you willing to be used by him?

Dear Lord, thank you that there's always a chance for a fresh start with you. I can leave my sins at the cross and receive forgiveness. Help me forgive myself for yesterday's mistakes and move forward with you.

SIXTEEN

My Forgiveness Story

MIRANDA J. CHIVERS

> Then Jesus said, "Father, forgive them, for they do not know what they do."
>
> —Luke 23:34

Do you struggle with forgiveness? We know holding grudges destroys our soul and impairs our relationships. But how can we forgive when the hurt was intentional or had profound consequences?

On the cross, Jesus told us the secret. Regardless of what others do to us, we must overcome the need for an apology and give the hurt to God. Forgiveness is one-sided. Although we may pray for resolution to the broken relationship or situation, forgiveness is about our own healing. It is letting go of the distress caused by the other person or situation. The damage may be irreversible, and the memory remains, but the pain lessens. We must understand that we cannot expect to have true intimacy with God until we learn to forgive.

I knew my marriage was over when I found the receipt for a very expensive pearl necklace in my husband's suit jacket. The letters in his briefcase told me about the recipient.

While he packed his things to move out, I was involved in a serious car accident. He never checked on my status at the hospital and ignored their pickup request. I called a friend to bring me home. His cruelty shocked me.

Over the next year, while I recovered at home and cared for my two children, the harassing and threatening phone calls from his girlfriend added to my trauma. And since she was a third party, my lawyer couldn't help me. In those days, verbal harassment and empty threats weren't crimes.

I feared losing my kids. My anxiety rose, and I spiralled into depression. My self-worth hit rock bottom. I'd suffered minor but permanent injuries in the accident, including brain trauma. I couldn't multi-task and had difficulties concentrating. I had to develop new methods to learn, cope and problem-solve. The game playing from my ex and his girlfriend, and the lack of legal clout added to the weight of my recovery.

Anger fueled my depression. Where was God in this catastrophe? In my despair, I felt abandoned and forgotten. I rebelled and ditched God. But my judgement was hampered. A sex trafficker seduced me. I needed help to get out. Then, I defied God further by marrying a man who used alcohol to cope with his resentments. We fed each other's anger, and my negativity worsened.

Fifteen years later, after a health crisis, I collapsed. Among other things, I was diagnosed with complex PTSD. Physically and mentally, I'd reached rock bottom. There was no way to go, but up. I reached out. And God answered.

Asking God for forgiveness was easier than forgiving my ex-husband and his partner. Our children suffered from the ongoing animosity. This affected our relationships too. My torch of hatred lit angry fires everywhere. I didn't know how to forgive nor how to heal.

When I discovered that I didn't need to hear any apologies or restore dysfunctional relationships, I realized that forgiveness wasn't about those who'd injured me. It was about me and my spiritual freedom. I needed to let go of the pain and ask God to mend my bruised heart.

The memories of deep hurt are not erased easily. Time doesn't always undo the sadness of some events. We can't undo the past. But we can embrace the future, knowing that God wants good for us. He will take our pain and make our life beautiful again. By giving up the grudges, we can experience happiness and enjoy full spiritual intimacy. Only then our heart will fully open to God's love and peace.

> *Dear Lord, I repent of holding grudges against (person's name). This habit has caused me to become bitter and unloving towards others. I now release this pain to you. Please heal my heart and help me find joy again.*

SEVENTEEN

In the Midst of it All

CJ WESTCOT

Today I decided to forgive you. Not because you apologized, or because you acknowledged the pain that you caused me, but because my soul deserves peace.

—Najwa Zebian

I was twelve. I wonder if that mattered to you.

I often think back on what it felt like laying there waiting to hear the creaking of your footsteps down the hallway. Your figure darkening the doorway. Your sister sleeping next to me. Unable to express the discomfort of the moment yet unwilling to tell anyone out of fear and embarrassment. Did it matter to you?

Did you grow up and think about me? I did. I thought about all the times you were there. I thought about the way I viewed intimacy and love. The snapshot my brain and body took that forever altered my perception of what I thought of my worth and what it meant to be with someone. I thought about the choices I made at 17. The people I sought after to help me feel complete and desired. Would it have been different if those nights at your sisters hadn't happened? Would I be different? My purity and innocence were gone. Only shame and brokenness remained.

I wish I could say that healing and forgiveness came easily. I'm 37, and it still takes my breath away. I have moments where I cry out to the Lord, "Tell me that I. AM. ENOUGH!" But it wasn't until a conversation with a friend one morning that I realized I haven't forgiven that pain that was caused so long ago. My friend chose to speak the truth over me that morning that I had refused to acknowledge. **After every moment of pain, every moment of abuse, every moment of shame, God can pick us up and we can find healing.**

But how could God help me heal? Why should I be expected to forgive? The response to my questions: GOD. IS. LOVE.

God doesn't want us to experience pain and heartbreak. He doesn't want us to be broken and feel shame. His deepest desire is that we would know that we are loved in every corner of our darkness. And he loves ALL. Even the ones who do the breaking.

So, how does God's presence in our most hurtful moments help us to forgive? Rather than being overwhelmed by shame and fear, we can instead be overwhelmed by HIM alone. We can look back and see God in our pain, loving us and calling us HIS. Telling us we are ENOUGH. We can be healed and therefore forgive because we recognize we are fully loved by

HIM. God is the one who will restore our brokenness, and HE will continue to love those who are lost.

We learn that by forgiving, we no longer give our deepest wounds power over our worth. We no longer identify as broken but find restoration through healing and the knowledge that there is no need to look for fulfillment with anyone or anything but GOD.

> *Father, I ask you to take our hurt. Take our anger and resentment and replace them with peace. Help us to forgive those who have brought us harm. Help us to let go, to allow your presence to fill us, reminding us that you are always there in the midst of it all. Father, we love you. Let us remember we are not alone on our journey to peace and forgiveness. Amen.*

CJ Westcot is a teacher and upcoming Christian Writer from North Mississippi. In 2019, while serving with a team in Los Angeles, God called her into ministry. Her heart for people who are hurting, and their stories of redemption are what drives her writing. CJ is passionate about walking alongside others in their journey and currently serves with the Desoto County Dream Center, writing devotionals and recording the life-changing stories of those in the community. Her desire is that people will feel encouraged by these stories and maybe find the strength one day to tell their own.

facebook.com/cjwestcot

EIGHTEEN

Healing through the Hurt

CJ WESTCOT

> "It is as though there is a splinter working its way to the surface, only this splinter is in your soul. And just as the skin wants a foreign object gone and pushes it out, the soul wants to be healthy and will not leave you in peace until you stop drenching it with the poisons of your feelings about the past."

—Stephen Mansfield

Many years ago when I was in college, I was mistreated by a boyfriend's parents because of the sins of my family. I distinctly remember sitting in their kitchen one weekend where I found myself alone with his mother. She turned in her chair and asked how serious I saw myself getting with her son. I thought the question strange because we had not really spoken about it between the two of us, so I told her I wasn't quite sure what she was asking.

She then told me that she was glad that we were having a good time together but that she didn't see it being long-term because we come from two different worlds. Confused and naïve, I asked what she meant. She proceeded to tell me that the events that lead to my parent's divorce are not something that she and her husband wanted their son to take into a relationship with a potential wife. To put it plainly, the fact that I came from a divorced home with an adulterous mother and a father with a checkered past made me unacceptable in their eyes.

I remember leaving that night wondering what I had done wrong. I thought I was doing everything right. We went to church together every weekend. We always sat with the door open and on opposite sides of the couch. We never showed public displays of affection. My boyfriend and I barely even held hands, yet my parent's divorce made me an unacceptable girlfriend?

For many years, I carried this hurt and with it unanswered questions. Did all "church" members view adultery, addiction, and divorce this way? What about grace? What about forgiveness? Isn't that what the bible teaches? Isn't that what God is supposed to be about? Why did my parent's choices make ME damaged?

It is sad that I allowed this single event to push me away from the church for over a decade. Then, one day in my early 30s, a friend took me to lunch, and we had an honest conversation about what it was doing to my heart to hold onto this bitterness. My negative views of people in the church and the sins of my parents were seeping into my personal life, all because I couldn't let go of one person's opinion.

My friend spoke biblical truth over me; recalling the parable of the unforgiving debtor in Matthew 18, where

Jesus teaches us to forgive from the heart. The lesson we must understand is that we ALL carry some form of brokenness and shame. Our views of one another must never overshadow the redemptive blood of Christ. Forgiveness should be what lives in our hearts, not anger and resentment of another's sins. By forgiving, we learn to heal wounds of the heart and gain the ability to love as Christ has called us to love his people.

Father, please forgive us for holding on to the hurt caused by others. Forgive us for the pain we cause when we choose bitterness over redemption. Father, you are the Great Healer and we ask that You whisper calm over our lives and remind us to choose love and forgiveness above all. Amen.

NINETEEN

Finding Grace in the Wounds

CJ WESTCOT

"Make peace with your broken pieces."

–R. H. Sin

It's midday in a dingy hotel room off the interstate. Her phone reads 5 missed calls, and she looks down to see he's calling again. She quickly dresses herself and attempts to repair her hair in the mirror before leaving the room. She knows when she walks out those doors she will be greeted by her biggest fear and her life will be forever changed. There is no running away from the problem, no escape. She must face her guilt and her shame head on. As she walks to her car, she can see the anger and the hurt across her husband's face. She whispers to herself, "God, forgive me."

God, forgive me.

So often, we speak these words in prayer. But do we truly accept and believe what we are asking from God or do we continue to allow the enemy to speak shame and condemnation over our hearts? **Why do we ask for forgiveness but refuse to walk in the truth that we are made clean by the cross?**

Early in my marriage I made personal choices that were not only dishonorable to the covenant I entered into with God but also to the vows I made to my husband. Being the one who inflicted these wounds is something I will always carry. Through many years of counseling, painful conversations, and making an intentional daily decision to be transparent with one another, hearing the words "I forgive you" was very humbling.

When we began the journey to restoration, I knew better than to think everything would be healed overnight. I knew that there would be days we'd have to endure pain as if salt had been poured into an open wound. But I took comfort in knowing we were making the conscious choice to fight for our marriage, together. No matter what.

Yet why, after all that we had been through, was I still choosing to condemn myself day after day? My husband could say, "I forgive you," yet I struggled to look at myself in the mirror. The enemy had a stronghold of my heart and he delighted in reminding me daily that I had invited him into my life once; what made me think I wouldn't allow him in again? The answer was clear.

THE CROSS.

Jesus did not pay for my sins so that I would carry guilt and condemnation from the past. He took on my sin so that I might live a life redeemed and be made whole. Through repentance, I would find judgement, NOT condemnation. The judgement for my sin is what holds

The Favor of Forgiveness

me accountable for my actions, but the Lord also offers me grace and mercy on the pathway to healing.

Rather than spending so much time allowing the enemy to breathe his lies over me, I learned to walk in the redemptive light of Christ. I found myself turning to John 8 and the story of the Woman Caught in Adultery. During those times when I question why such a good Father would forgive, I read and speak these words over my life:

"Where are your accusers? Didn't even one of them condemn you?"

"No, Lord," she said.

And Jesus said, "Neither do I."

> Father, thank you for the grace and mercy you freely offer. It is through Your sacrifice that we find forgiveness. Thank you for showing us we can be made whole in Jesus. Father, we love you. Amen.

TWENTY

Where Is God When Others Hurt Us?

TANYA DUFFEY

"And we know that for those who love God all things work together for good, for those who are called according to his purpose."

—Romans 8:28

The hurts others may have put on you can change you in a way that causes you to be more effective for Christ.

Let's be honest, hurts... hurt... And even worse, what if it was someone from the church? Someone you trusted? Someone who claimed to be a Christian? I know friend, I have been there too. But please do not allow someone else who has hurt you to keep you away from His love, His peace, His joy, and the life He has waiting for you. That would be devastating.

If we allow it to, that hurt will grow inside of us and keep us from living the life God has planned. Why in the world would we give someone that kind of power over our lives???

We mature when we forgive without the apology or acknowledgement.

We are able to move forward and heal when we choose forgiveness. It is one of our greatest strengths. I love this verse in Jeremiah 29: 13 "You will seek Me and find Me when you search for Me with all your heart". It's a promise that when we look into his words (the Bible) and truly with an open heart seek Him, we will find Him. It's one of life's sweetest miracles. I remember a time in my life when someone in authority within the church hurt me and my family so badly that I thought I would never be able to trust the church again. It caused me to question "Why would you allow this to happen, Lord?" One thing I realized during this time was that what the enemy uses to destroy you, God allows because he knows he can trust you to do the right thing! He is using these moments to make you stronger for His purpose in your life. When we see it this way, we can understand more clearly. The hurts others may have put on you can change you in a way that causes you to be more effective for Christ! These verses remind us where to keep our focus and trust... Matthew 5: 44, "But I say to you, Love your enemies and pray for those that persecute you." Romans 8: 28, "And we know that for those who love God all things work together for good, for those who are called according to his purpose."

> *Lord, help us forgive others who have hurt us not because they deserve it or that they even care, but because we deserve to heal and move on to what you have planned for our lives. As we let go and allow you to have your way in each circumstance, may we see more clearly the way that you see*

things. Help us to pray for those that have hurt us; that they may know you. Amen

---

Writing has been a lifelong must for as long as Tanya can remember. The stacks of journals, post-it notes, and random notepads filling her closet attest to this truth. She published her first newsletter in 200, a monthly newsletter to encourage moms on their faith journey. Tanya regularly has her work published in GO! Christian magazine and has been a contributor to several online magazines.

When I'm not writing, you can often find me curled up with a good book and a gigantic cup of coffee, hanging out with my husband and two children, homeschooling, or getting outside to be in nature. I write devotionals based on real-life issues and have recently fallen in love with writing poetry. My hope and prayer is that people have a place to come, quiet the noise and hear His voice. I'd love to connect with you on my blog or Facebook page.

http://thejourney-home.com/

TWENTY-ONE

Shedding the Weight

ROBERT KAPEN

> "Be kind and compassionate to one another, forgiving each other, just as in Christ God forgave you."
>
> –Ephesians 4:32

The idea of forgiveness and an apology are similar and necessary with a little bit of difference. By saying, "I'm sorry," to a person you have wronged or hurt, you are acknowledging that you did something to make them feel negatively. Forgiveness is the other side of the coin. Someone has wronged or hurt you. It begins affecting your life, so you may confront or converse with this person, or you may just forgive them in your heart. You're able to say (at least to yourself), "Hey, this action hurt me, but I don't want to give it anymore time and energy. I forgive you!"

Both terms need actions attached. Saying, "I'm sorry," means you are verbally saying you vow to change your actions so you don't have to feel those negative emotions in future situations. Forgiving someone is again someone wronged or hurt you, it affects your emotions and you don't want to carry that weight anymore, so you forgive them. The action is releasing that feeling so you don't have to treat them any differently or without any animosity compared to how you might treat anyone else. But, releasing the feeling allows you to knock off the weight and life draining fruits it's most likely causing in your life. If you don't, over time, that weight starts to grow and develop harmful fruits like anger, jealousy, hate, pride, and coveting. I think that is why God told us clear misunderstandings quickly because He knows what they will become if we let them simmer. Unforgiveness will grab on tightly and produce ungodly fruits which will cause separation between us and Him. As illustrated in James 1, sin gives birth to more sin and then ultimately death. Unforgiveness will only grow if you let it until it brings death.

I have seen the ill effects of not apologizing and unforgiveness in my own marriage. After a normal argument, the situation can quickly become a big blow out if we don't expediently apologize to each other. There is nothing better for a marriage, besides God, than forgiveness. When people ask, "what's the secret to marriage?" my go-to response is, "Two things: 1. Don't be afraid to say 'sorry.' 2. Always be willing to forgive the other person." When you do those two things it levels the playing field. It puts you in a humble stance among God, you, and your partner. It's hard to be mad at a sincerely humble person. It's also a good reminder to ourselves that we're not gods, and we're not perfect. So, we need help from the One who is: Christ, our Lord and Savior.

There's another action you must do to genuinely forgive someone or apologize to them: humble yourself before God and that person. When we release the pain, anger, and unforgiveness in the backdrop of what Jesus did for us, it seems like such a minute gesture. Compare that relationship to our relationship with God, we need to realize how many times God has forgiven us and continues to extend that grace to our neighbors.

God, please expose and bring to light the areas we need to apologize and forgive, and by doing so, You will get all the glory. I pray we drop all our pride, and You will continue to supply us with comfort and strength.

I'm Robert Kapen, and I grew up and live in Los Angeles. I've been married 5+ years. I used to live a healthy life mentoring youth through YoungLife until college when I contracted an unknown virus that left me paralyzed and mute. I found healing in writing, so I combined it with my love for youth and wrote a youth devo called Kapen: Yells of a Young Man, available on Amazon. Now I spend my days deeply loving God.

TWENTY-TWO

Forgiveness, Humility, & Repentance

CHARIS MUSICK

"And when you pray, make sure you forgive the faults of others so that your Father in heaven will also forgive you. But if you withhold forgiveness from others, your Father withholds forgiveness from you."

—Matthew 6:14-15 (TPT)

In life, we are given many opportunities to practice two important disciplines: repentance and forgiveness. Scripture speaks on both. Paul in Acts 20:21 writes about his testifying about repentance—meaning to make a 180° turn from what you were doing and refocus on Jesus; to change your mind—and faith, even after being plotted against by the Jews. Prior to that, Matthew speaks about forgiving others so that you will be forgiven (6:14).

While "forgive and forget" has no biblical support, I do believe in practicing forgiveness and aiming to live unoffendable, choosing to not let offense and bitterness poison my heart. In the heat of racial tensions in the summer of 2020, I was invited into many conversations with pastors and friends where I shared my few experiences with racism as a black woman. I encouraged them to not stop with me but to keep seeking to hear real stories of people of color. Amid sharing my life and childhood growing up in southeast Louisiana and my journey through Texas to Missouri, I received messages from 2 different old high school classmates. I didn't remember needing to forgive, so I also didn't know my heart needed an apology, until I received these messages just hours apart:

> "Hi Charis, I know this message is out of the blue, but I need to tell you something. I'm sorry for some things that I said to you when we were back in high school. I was one of those people who said that you were really white on the inside, and I'm so ashamed that I ever thought it was okay to say that to you. You are such a beautiful person and I have always admired you. I was so ignorant, and wrong to say that to you, and I'm truly so sorry".

> "First off I want to apologize to you. I am sorry. I don't know how far this goes back for you but I do know you dealt with it in high-school. I remember how kids would describe you being a "white girl trapped in a black girl's body". I know you laughed it off but those words are hurtful and I was a part of that problem. I am TRULY sorry."

I read and sobbed after receiving each message. My heart was caught off guard by their words and their power after 12+ years since these experiences.

A couple days later, I had lunch with a girlfriend from church. After lunch, we sat in her car and she looked into my eyes, held my hand, and cried as she repented to me for the years of hurtful, racist things said or done against me or my family. She hadn't done anything herself, but she repented on behalf of those who have, whether intentionally or unintentionally. I sobbed as she prayed for me, for us, for our country, for the Church. It was such a holy moment of unity, healing, and humility... and, friends, it's just the beginning.

> *Even if I never receive an apology for wrongs committed against me, Father, I repent for withholding forgiveness from those You love. I invite You, Holy Spirit, to heal the broken places in my heart and reveal those I need to repent to. Help me choose obedience, forgiveness, and humility, choosing repentance, making You the object of my focus and all my desires. I pray I would seek to "if possible, as far as it depends on [me], live at peace with everyone" (Romans 12:18 CSB). Father, I thank You. Jesus, I love You. Holy Spirit, I welcome You. Amen.*

Charis Musick is a writer, coffee shop enthusiast, and lover of quality conversations. She started a new blog, *Adventure On*, when she and her husband, Mason, moved to Missouri from Texas. Originally about adapting to a new place, the blog became the written documentation through her journey with infertility, grief after losses, and life in general. As an outcome of walking through hardship with the Lord, Charis is passionate about genuinely championing others with hope, joy, encouragement, and truth to pursue wholeness in body, mind, and soul.

Charis and Mason are college sweethearts who have been married since May 2013. Documenting their lives in words and photos, Charis and Mason are committed to every twist, turn, ascent, and descent the adventure ahead holds.

charismusick.com

TWENTY-THREE

Healing Our Woundedness

TAMBRY HARRIS

"We are all wounded in some way. What we do with our woundedness defines us. If we learn and grow from our wounds, they can motivate us to claim our Going-Forward Story."

–From ***Awakening the Light,*** Tambry Harris

All of us have more than likely been wounded by another person in our lifetime. Culturally, many of us are raised to be tough and push down the feelings of hurt within us. Somehow, we feel stronger by burying the pain. Yet, in reality we are binding the hurt and the pain deep within, never allowing the wound to breathe and heal, only to have it fester underneath or harden into a protective shell.

My story includes being wounded as a child in a family who were distracted by their own trauma; they could not or did not come to my aid. My paternal grandparents were killed by a drunk driver before I was born. My father was kept away in the Vietnam war and didn't meet me until I was six months old. Compound these events with death coming early in the form of cancer on my mother's side of the family. Two uncles were diagnosed in their twenties and died in their thirties. An older cousin battled leukemia when young only to be killed in a freak automobile accident at age 16. It seemed we barely made it through one tragedy when another would arrive, leaving no time to mourn. When families are reeling from heartache and overwhelm, sexual predators have a way of finding their way to their victim. That was the case for me as a precious girl around the age of five. For years to come, the hurt little girl inside me felt anger about the violation as well as betrayal by the adults around her.

Anger and resentment can be part of what feels like a protective shell, and yet it traps the festering pain within. My protective shell was thick and held me together, but it also kept the pain inside and the joy outside. Does this sound familiar? Have you built up a thick shell to protect that wounded part but are keeping out some of the most important things in life?

Know this is not what God would want for you. You were designed to have feelings, to feel joy, and to love fully. So, how do you release the hurt and embrace the good?

First, you breathe deeply. As you breathe, invite Spirit into your heart and soul. For me, it is helpful to breathe in, "Holy One", and breathe out "heal me." If you have a special name for God, use that word. Sit with the breath coming in, filling your lungs, settling your body.

Try to visualize where the pain resides within you; breathe into that space. Some feel the pain, wound, or anger in their shoulders, others their chest and others in their stomach. For me, it seems to reside in my shoulders and my neck. As I breathe in, I visualize the air flowing to that space and almost expanding the area. With my exhale, I see my shoulders settling and releasing. Many times, just three deep breaths are enough to help my body release the tension and pain I hold.

As you inhale, breathe in God's love and healing power. As you exhale, seek to breathe out the anger and resentment. Continue to do this and notice if it helps to relax your body and spirit.

Next, name the pain or wounds that need to be healed to overcome the restrictive shell you have built. This may be the first time you have named that person or event that hurt you deeply. If you feel tension or uneasiness, invite God to sit with you in the naming and claiming. Know that you are not alone.

As you become clear around the pain and woundedness, allow that to formulate into a healing prayer or healing intention. Offer this prayer to God who can be your loving, healing partner.

My personal life scripture is, *"For I know the plans that I have for you," declares the Lord, "plans to prosper you and not to harm you, plans to give you hope and a future."* Jeremiah 29:11. May this be your prayer:

Holy One, I know you have special plans for me. The woundedness that I feel is not of you. Please fill my spirit and help me release the pain and anger that I have been holding so that I can experience the hope and future you have for me and my life. Amen.

Tambry Harris found her voice, named her truth and created a vision to help others who have experienced the pain and shame of trauma and abuse find healing, strength and freedom. She believes that as we make our own wounds visible and available, they can be of service to the healing of others. This story of wounding, struggle, and healing encourages survivors to claim their going-forward stories. Tambry's experiences, concepts and heart shine light into the darkness that surrounds sexual abuse.

Tambry has a Master's Degree in Applied Psychology and certifications in the areas of Leadership Coaching, Spiritual Direction, Change Management and Diversity. Through her organization, Going Forward: Survivors to Thrivers, she provides Individual Guidance, Retreats and Speaking Engagements to bring awareness and light into the shame, silence and darkness of sexual abuse.

Find more writing on Amazon and visit
survivorstothrivers.com

TWENTY-FOUR

Between Friends

LEENA J

"And if you stand praying, if you hold anything against anyone, forgive them, so that your Father in heaven may forgive you your sins."

–Mark 11:25

From the time I first learned about forgiveness in Sunday school, I always regarded it with some skepticism. Apart from relishing the truth of our Heavenly Father forgiving our sins, I was hard-pressed to find examples of it in daily life. From my observations, it appeared that forgiveness was shorthand for "unresolved anger barely masked until the justice of karma prevails."

In my twenties however, God gave me a deeper, more personal understanding of forgiveness in a way I never expected. My best friend, who was also my informal spiritual advisor, revealed that she was in love with my ex-boyfriend of three days, and promptly started dating him. Awkward? Yes. For *her*. But for me, it was absolutely devastating. My ex and I been together for a number of years by then, and my BFF/mentor was the only person who knew my long, complex history with him. To say that her announcement was a turning point in our friendship is an understatement. We tried to maintain something of our close rapport, but it was irrevocably changed.

Before long, I could feel myself slipping into depression. She and I hardly talked anymore, and other mutual friends were visibly uncomfortable around us. Regardless of how I was feeling, I made a decision... almost naively. I decided to forgive her. It was not a decision made with grace. I wish I could say it was. It was a decision made in desperation and fear. I needed to survive the visceral anguish, and something inside of me knew I would only be free from it if I forgave. I also knew that I was *called* to forgive, and I didn't want God to hold it against me if I didn't. To heal, I allowed myself time to grieve the loss of this seminal friendship and reflected daily on Scriptures teachings on forgiveness, processing the journey in words:

Forgiveness is simple, a relinquishing.

Forgiveness is complex, a commitment to release through clenched fists.

Forgiveness is a promise, a pledge to free and be freed.

Forgiveness is offensive, an affront to my sense of justice.

Forgiveness is a threat, an assault on my right for revenge.

Forgiveness is heavy, lovely in theory, and wrenching in reality.

Forgiveness is essential, the entrance to the pathway of restoration.

Fast forward to 2021...that BFF and ex are now married and have a family of their own. She and I have also reconnected, which has been a lovely surprise. My heart is full of gratitude for our Father who, in His wisdom and timing, restored my heart and is now quietly stitching together a renewed friendship.

Are you walking through the terrain of forgiveness? Keep going friend, and remember that you do not travail alone. Capture your journey of forgiveness in a way that speaks to you. Let it become a keepsake of God's faithfulness over your life and evidence of the Enemy's loss. Above all, allow yourself to be loved through it all...you are worthy of it.

Professionally, I help edit a small academic journal and have taught courses at both the undergraduate and graduate level. Before that, I was a graphic designer for a number of years. And I've always always written...even if it was just in private journals. Writing has been a source of comfort in times of distress, clarity in times of confusion, and an outlet for...well...life.

Personally, I love learning and deeply connecting with people. So as I navigate my way through this second phase of life, during a pandemic no less, I'll try to share things that I hope will give you a chuckle or inspire a meaningful pause on your journey too.

reveleena.com

TWENTY-FIVE

Hearts Can Change

MATEJA STOLNIK VUGREK

"Be kind and compassionate to one another, forgiving each other, just as in Christ God forgave you."

—Ephesians 4:32 (NIV)

We live in an upside-down world, as we see how very strange it is. We have a lot of troubles. Many of us are aware that we do not live in a normal and perfect world like our Father originally planned. Sin entered the stage, and we live with consequences daily. On top of that, we are living in a spiritual battle. Love and hate, evil and good, forgiveness and unforgiveness are in battling one another.

This war is exhausting, it can play with our minds and hearts. Because of sin, people tend to hurt people.

When He went back to Heaven, He promised to give us the Holy Spirit as a Helper. We have been given another chance; we have been forgiven; and He gave us a new life and a gift. When I think about that, it is almost impossible to comprehend that somebody forgave me from all my sins and went a step further—suffering enormous pain—and died for me. Wow! There is no one else who would sacrifice so much and die for us.

On that cross, He showed perfect love and forgiveness. As I was thinking about this, I became ashamed because I did not completely forgive some people that have hurt me. Somebody from my close family has hurt me and that was more painful than anything. I thought, "Oh I can forgive everything but not that, that person is not deserving my forgiveness, it is too painful."

Before my father became a Christian, he was unfaithful to my mother. First, I did not think about forgiveness, but I only thought about how he hurt my family and me. My pain was deep, and I thought that could only happen to others, not me.

But as I was searching for God and His direction, His words came to me more alive than ever before. He told me, reminded me, and whispered to my heart those words: "My precious daughter, you know and remember how my Son was betrayed by his very best friends: friends he considered family, to whom he gave his time and love. He gave them everything you can imagine someone could give." Unfortunately, that was still not enough for them. He was so compassionate that he forgave them, died for them, and loved them.

When we think about this truth, our hearts can change, and we can have a Kingdom perspective.

Today, God is not asking us to go to the cross, but He is asking us to come closer to Him, learn from Him and His words. Even when we feel we cannot forgive, He is faithful and will come alongside us. Our Helper, the Holy Spirit, will remind us of the words of the Bible. Our hearts cannot be the same if we trust Him. When we need to step and forgive, He will give us strength and love we thought we could not have. He will go with us to that place of forgiveness.

> *Our Father in heaven we are so thankful that you showed us a perfect example of what compassionate love looks like. You forgave us first, died for us, and showed us unconditional love. We ask you that You will always direct our steps, help us to forgive, and heal our hearts. Your love is sufficient for us and we believe that we can do everything through Your son.*

Mateja Stolnik Vugrek is an editor of a Christian magazine for youth. With her husband and their missionary friend, they run a Christian non-profit organization with lots of children and youth camps. Their dream is to help children and youth discover their potential for a life full of purpose and love. Mateja loves books, reading, writing and researching, cooking, and walks in nature with her husband and friends. Also, she loves everything sweet and needs to always finish her meal with some kind of dessert. Her passions are children and youth. She is about to publish her first Children's book and plans to publish more books and touch many hearts with them.

TWENTY-SIX

The Prison of Unforgiveness

KATIE ARTHUR

"Here's what unforgiveness does to us. It makes us irrational. It puts us in a state of vengeful frenzy where we don't even see that it stopped being about justice a long time ago."

—Tim Mackie

In Matthew 18, Jesus tells The Parable of the Unforgiving Servant. The servant owed the king a massive debt he was unable to pay. The king ordered that he and his family be sold to pay it off. The servant pleaded with the king who chose to forgive the debt. The servant then went out to a man who owed him a miniscule debt he couldn't pay. The servant had him thrown in prison. Upon hearing this, the king was angry and had the servant thrown in jail until he could pay the debt he had previously been forgiven.

A lot is packed into this parable; however, I want to focus on one detail - location. When the servant went to the king and couldn't pay his debt, the king was going to sell him to work it off. The king was sentencing the servant to face the natural consequences of his debt. At that time and in that culture this meant he would be sold into debt slavery and work until he could pay off what was owed. We see a huge contrast in the sentence the servant gives to the man who owes him. The servant throws this man in prison until he can pay his debt. Do you see the problem? The man cannot work to pay off the debt from prison. He is essentially sentenced to a life in prison where what is owed will never be paid.

When I approach someone who has wronged me with unforgiveness in my heart, I lose sight entirely of what would even be fair or just. In my unforgiveness, I place those that wronged me in a prison where I don't allow them the opportunity to change or apologize. As I imprison them, I imprison myself, cutting myself off from receiving what my heart longs for: to receive what is owed - an apology, a recognition of the wrong done to me. This vengeful chaining is part of human nature.

So, how do we escape this prison? In Matthew 18, before The Parable of the Unforgiving Servant, Jesus provides a perfect escape plan. He teaches us to approach our offender and tell them their faults - first alone, then with another, then with the church or wider body of believers. When we tell them of their fault, we offer them the opportunity to recognize and address their wrongs. By not sentencing them to punishment, we extend forgiveness while having the opportunity to receive an apology and have things be righted between us.

Now, just because someone is given the opportunity to right their wrongs doesn't mean they will. Jesus gives us permission to let those who offend us face the natural consequences of their actions and be released from the fellowship of believers. We remain responsible to continue to live with forgiveness in our heart toward them, freeing them from the shackles of unforgiveness with the opportunity to recognize what they have done wrong and pay the debt that is owed.

Jesus, soften my heart toward those who have offended me. Grant me the ability to extend forgiveness toward them and open the door for them to recognize and right their wrongs. And, if they do not right their wrongs, teach me to continue to walk in forgiveness toward them still. Amen.

Find out more about Katie at
https://themismatchedwife.com/

TWENTY-SEVEN

The Forgiveness Quandary

ERIN WATSON MOHR

"And when you pray, make sure you forgive the faults of others so that your Father in heaven will also forgive you."

–Matthew 6:14

Forgiveness is such a controversial topic. I pastored at a church for twenty years and spent many sessions with different individuals who came to me regarding the issue of forgiveness.

Although they would be sharing their confidential life struggles with me, thinking that what they needed was prayer or deliverance but what I detected was the underlying circumstances at the root of their problem…unforgiveness.

It wasn't until I asked the question have you forgiven (insert name) or forgiven yourself for what occurred, that they would have a lightbulb moment, an aha of revelation that perhaps deep down beneath the surface of their current mess was actually the root of unforgiveness. Most often the answer to my question was a resounding "no."

I would then suggest that we take time to pray about this need for inner heart healing. Oftentimes I was met with the typical answer of "I can't do that," or "they don't deserve to be forgiven." The subject was met with resistance due to a distorted perception of what forgiveness is actually about.

My genuine responses were always directing back to their need to do it for themself, that forgiveness is not an action that one is deserving of or earns brownie points over time in order to be worthy of receiving it. Forgiveness is an inner choice to set oneself free from the control of a past experience. Forgiveness is about the individual themself. When unforgiveness is present it is like a prison that is around oneself and easily sustained until the choice to forgive is reached. Then it is like the bars of imprisonment come crashing down releasing the captive from their unsuspecting torment.

Quite often our emotions lead the choice and get in the way from us making progress. I always say that the action proceeds the healing. The choice must first be established and then the emotions will follow suit eventually. Only we ourselves hold the key to lead us into that freedom that we were designed to live in.

The Bible states very clearly that we are to forgive others for their faults. This does not mean their weaknesses which are so readily noticeable. (Might I add that we all have our areas of weakness that are most often our blind spots.) This refers to the action acted out, or the words that were spoken, whichever the affliction that was unleashed against us.

When we choose to withhold this foundational value, we actually cut ourselves off from receiving forgiveness from our Heavenly Father, and we also build those invisible prison walls around ourselves.

I encourage each of us to never let our emotions be the guide by which we are led to choose. Forgiveness is a powerful choice of unlocking our freedom and I for one, want to live free.

> *Father God, I thank you that you paid the price once and for all for my sins with your shed blood upon the cross. I come to you today and surrender the burden of unforgiveness that I have been unnecessarily carrying upon myself as dead weight. I release myself from this pain and I ask that you pour out your healing upon me as I forgive * (insert name) for (name the action) that was committed against me. I choose to set myself free from the prison of unforgiveness. Thank you for setting me free! In your most gracious name Jesus I pray, Amen.*

*Please insert your own name if you need to forgive yourself for choices you have made. Sometimes we neglect to see that we actually need to let ourselves off the hook (the one we hung ourselves upon) for disappointments that stem from inside that lead to us making some unhealthy choices.

Find more works by Erin on Amazon and visit
www.emergecoaching.ca

TWENTY-EIGHT

The Spiraled Path of Forgiveness

DVORA ELISHEVA

"He leads me in paths of righteousness for His name's sake."

—Psalm 23:3

Literal Hebrew: "He leads/guides me in circular paths of righteousness for His name's sake"

There are eight different words for "path" in Hebrew. I am surprised by King David's choice: *ma'ageleh tzedek* (paths of righteousness). That word, *"ma'ageleh"* speaks of circles and my mind's eye envisions flowing spirals of righteousness rising ever upward. What are these paths? Pondering this picture and the season before me, I recall God's forgiveness. A terrible awareness of my sin finds comfort and hope in His forgiveness, which is not based on a day of fasting, prayer, and good deeds weighed against bad, but rather on the costly atoning blood of Jesus. Having received such grace, how can I not extend it to others?

Then reality sets in. Perhaps you know what I mean; that endless cycle, battling to forgive. For me it was the hurt inflicted by my best friend, Esti. A misunderstanding escalated to a harsh exchange of words that left us both feeling shattered and broken – though at the time I was only aware of my own pain. It would be months of wrestling in prayer and meditating on verses like *a "friend loves forever"* (Proverbs 17:17), and *"love one another as I have loved you"* (John 13:34) before I yielded, said the words, and prayed that my heart and feelings would align with forgiveness. I meant it, but then a memory, or a chance word would sidetrack me, sometimes – months or years later. Caught up short, I would cry out to the Lord, "Haven't I walked this path before? I thought I'd forgiven her. Why are those feelings still there?" In my pain I found an amazing reassurance, yes, I had forgiven Esti, but something deeper connected with that pain or memory had been uncovered by God's spirit. Yes, I forgave *that*, but now darkness had been revealed what I hadn't seen before. It is *this* He was asking me to deal with now. God's "paths" of righteousness, actually moving me ever upward, higher, and closer to His righteousness. Little did I know that our friendship would end at an airport, some 15 years later, weeping in each other's arms as we said a final goodbye before Esti died of cancer three months later. Without that forgiveness lived out on the spiraled road of forgiveness, we never would have talked on the phone the day before she died. "My work is done," she barely was able to say, "Write Debbie; write your book." And I did.

When it comes to forgiveness, do you, like me, sometimes feel like you are dealing with the same thing, over and over again? Don't be discouraged. Jesus is simply asking you to receive His forgiveness and then extend it to others more deeply, more fully, more freely, bringing you into a place where, one day, when the scar is touched, the only response is love, not hurt, and forgiveness is fully actualized.

> *Jesus, thank you that forgiveness is a process. Thank you that when I first said, "I forgive ____," it was real. Thank you that when I struggle with that same issue, you are simply being my Good Shepherd, gently leading me in righteousness along Your wonderful spiraled path of forgiveness, drawing me higher and closer to You, and teaching me to forgive and love more deeply.*

Deborah Hemstreet writes under the pen name Dvora Elisheva. Find more on Amazon.

TWENTY-NINE

Confession

CARRIE BEVELL PARTRIDGE

"Therefore, confess your sins to one another, and pray for one another so that you may be healed."

—James 5:16

I had *completely* lost it with my seven-year-old son. Over what? He told me he didn't know how to turn the shower on by himself, but I knew that he could. It had already been a long day, and I was in a hurry to leave the house to meet my friends for coffee. I needed a break from my children, and I was worn out by their neediness that day.

So when my son whined and said he couldn't turn on the shower by himself, it triggered a really ugly response in me. Like yelling-and-jumping-up-and-down ugly. I am not a yeller, and I'm even less of a jump-up-and-downer, but I had reached the end of my rope that day. It was one of the most shameful responses I've given as a parent. My son cried, I cried, my daughters peeked out at me cautiously from behind their bedroom door... It was a mess, and I knew immediately that I would need to make things right by confessing my sin to my children and asking them to forgive me.

And I did. After I calmed down, I looked at their concerned little faces and told them how wrong it was for me to behave that way. I apologized to each of them and asked for their forgiveness, which they freely gave. We hugged, and I cried some more. The beauty of being freely forgiven, when you know you don't deserve it, is overwhelming.

You might've noticed that I said this was "*one* of the most shameful responses I've given as a parent." That's because, I'm sorry to say, there have been *many* shameful responses from me over my 20+ years of parenting five kids. It would be easy for me to explain away each response as being something my children drove me to and/or deserved, instead of taking ownership of my sin. But if I did that, I would be stunting my own spiritual growth as well as the growth of my children, since they learn by watching me and my responses.

Each time I humble myself by admitting my sin against my children, they are learning from my example that when we sin against someone, we need to make it right. It is hard--*really hard!*--, but it is necessary for restored relationships with each other and with God. And the more we practice it, the more natural it will become. This is a huge life lesson that begins in the safety of home but then extends into relationships outside of the home. And that is a gift!

Parents, let's not neglect this important lesson that our children learn through our example. Let's use our own needs for confession and forgiveness as teachable moments.

> *Father, thank You for Your promise to forgive us every time we confess our sins to you. Help us to humble ourselves and be obedient to confess to others when we have sinned against them, as well. Help us to live freely and fully from Your grace so that we will forgive others when they sin against us, just as we ourselves have been forgiven.*

Find more from Carrie at carriebevellpartridge.com.

THIRTY

Lament. Accept. Then Forgive.

NATALIE K. PICKERING, PHD, BCC, MISCP

"Forgiving is the only way to heal the wounds of a past we cannot change and cannot forget. Forgiving changes a bitter memory into a grateful memory, a cowardly memory into a courageous memory, and an enslaved memory into a free memory. Forgiving restores a self-respect that someone killed. And, more than anything else, forgiving gives birth to hope for the future after our past illusions have been shattered…When we forgive, we take God's hand, walk through the door, and stroll into the possibilities that wait for us to make them real."

—Lewis Smedes, *The Art of Forgiving*

As a psychologist I have journeyed with many women through painful stories to forgiveness. Mothers, daughters, wives, grandmothers, and friends have shared tragedies of war, disaster, abuse, regrets, and mistakes with depth of pain and anger, swirling fear and shame.

They are a mother who received a benign and unknowingly last *"Give me a call"* text from her young adult daughter whom she found lifeless to suicide the next day; she is a young woman with hopes of having her own family waking up in the post-operative bay to the reality that the wrong medical chart and procedure have left her infertile; and the wife who discovered last evening her husband's affair which she recounts with gut-wrenching sobs of betrayal trauma.

The unforgiveness and accompanying bitterness come in many forms- vows to never marry or love again, bitter rage, emotional walls, holding others at great distance, berating self with the tyranny of hindsight bias and harboring a growing chasm with God.

When the pain and silence and distance become too great, however, the cautious, begrudging, desperate work begins. Women reach out because they can't hold down a job, can't maintain a relationship, can't sleep, and realize that life is rushing by while their energies are consumed with nursing painfully infected wounds.

As women slowly, painfully share their stories – sometimes with words and sometimes without—there unfolds a new and deeper realization of the *Bigger Story*- the Creation, Fall, Redemption *Story* that encompasses hers. This *Story* is **not** to the exclusion of the vital recounting of loss and however long the recounting takes. Scripture honors the hurt. Lament (Ps 102:1-2; Lam 1:1; Jer 9:10) recounts and details with tears and fury and question the layers and ripples of loss impact. Scripture describes this,

"I am weak...my bones are in agony. I am sick at heart. How long, O Lord, until you restore me? I am worn out from sobbing..." (Ps 6:2-6).

As we lament, we can start to reconsider the *Ultimate Sacrifice and Loss* (Matt 27:32-56), a Loving Father watching his perfect Son die a horrific, innocent death. This fellowship of suffering (Phil 3:10) that Christ's humanity gifts us is our knowing that he can understand the depths of our pain (Mk 14:36).

As lament and loss make way for renewed hope in a knowing Savior, then we can dip a toe in accepting again the reality of unmet longings and recounting our eternal, awaiting pain-free *Home*. We hold the tension of loss and longing with the hope of no more pain (Rev 21:4) and justice realized (Deut 32:4). Honoring loss makes acceptance possible.

And then: forgiveness. Never easy, but possible, in the realized strength, power and example of our Father and His Son. We choose forgiveness rooted in recovered hope, validated loss, and reminder of the *Bigger Story*. We forgive as our Father gently reminds us that we have been forgiven and that our liberation from the poison of unforgiving bitterness, resentment, grudges against self and other, is truly possible even now, as we live in light of the freedom of forgiveness while looking towards *Home*.

> Have you honored the loss behind your resentment, anger, pain, and unforgiveness? Reflect on the passages noted above. Write a prayer or a psalm of lament of your very own. Pour out your heart to God

sharing every feeling, detail, and longing from your experience- honoring what has been lost. As you clear space for consideration of forgiveness, invite him to remind you of his presence, then and now.

Find more about Natalie at yourhighestplace.com.

THIRTY-ONE

Joseph: A Picture of God's Process

CLARE JOHNSON

"As for you, you intended evil against me, but God meant it for good."

—Genesis 50:20

It's likely that Joseph's father never discovered that his brothers had thrown Joseph into a pit, planned to kill him, and then sold him into slavery. We never read of a conversation between Jacob and any of his sons regarding their past offense.

Assuming that Joseph never told his Father what his brothers had done, what a great picture of God's love toward us that Joseph forgave them that completely! How was Joseph able to forgive his brothers of such cruel, heartless treatment? Could you forgive family members that betrayed you so deeply and coldheartedly sold you into slavery?

Perhaps a reason Joseph could forgive them is that he believed God was using his circumstances to accomplish

His purposes. Evidence of Christian maturity is the ability to remember God's ways are not our ways; we cannot judge God for what He allows in our lives. In our human understanding, we would protect Joseph from his hardship. We would save him from his brother's betrayal, pull him from the pit, seek his deliverance from enslavement, and defend him from being unjustly imprisoned. We cannot know the end result of what God is doing until He is finished.

By the time Joseph and his brothers were reunited, he didn't blame them. He had come to understand that every unjust circumstance God had allowed was a tool to accomplish His will in Joseph's life so he could say, *"You intended evil against me, but God meant it for good"*. He had peace regarding everything he endured, including slavery, false accusation, and imprisonment.

God used these trials to work in his heart and build intimacy and trust; as Joseph surrendered his heart to God in the process, he was prepared for his destiny as second in authority in Egypt. Did you get that? God used other people's abuse, lies, and false accusations to prepare Joseph for his calling.

This is a nugget of truth, although not easy to accept, that can transform us if we can wrap our head around it; every enemy, every difficult person, every hurtful circumstance, every rejection, every trauma, every challenge, and opposition is God's tool He has allowed to bring us closer to Him, transform us into His image, mold our character, and mature and prepare us for our specific calling. God never causes evil, but he allows it to work gold in our hearts and lives, if we allow Him.

What a victory if we can come to the place of thankfulness for even the unjust things that have happened to us because we believe that God allowed them for His purposes.

Joseph didn't know his release from prison was near; He had no idea that in one day he would go from prison to palace. No wilderness lasts forever; ours won't either. As we give God our "yes" in the process, there will come a time when our preparation has ended and we are ready to be released into that which God has prepared for us.

> *Heavenly Father, as we pour our hearts out before You, we thank You for filling us with Your peace. Thank You that You will help us to forgive those who have hurt us and release anything we hold against them to You, trusting that You alone can bring justice in our lives. We entrust our lives to You believing that You will use all things for our good. In Jesus name, Amen.*

Find more writings by Clare on Amazon.

Free Devotionals and Stories

Want a copy of a Devo Writers Collaboration for free?!

Go to ***read.ChristWriters.com***

Subscribe to get:

- a Devo Writers Collaboration ebook
- author interviews and special offers
- invitations to participate however you'd like (even voting on new topics and covers)
- links to more free books

Are YOU a writer?

Whether you've never written or you want to grow your author backlist, YOU can join the next collaboration book! Go to DevoWriters.com to learn more.

Check out the Facebook Group, Devo Writers Collaborations to follow along and see how you can contribute:

> facebook.com/groups/christiancollections

If you're an author and have any self-publishing needs, contact michael@michaellacey.me.

Last Request

The more reviews, the more readers we can attract. The more readers, the more we can advance the Kingdom and grow the Church in number and depth.

Your help means SO much; please leave an honest review on Amazon!

Thank you!

Made in the USA
Columbia, SC
28 November 2021